the guide to owning a
Bearded Dragon

David Zoffer & Tom Mazorlig

T.F.H. Publications, Inc.
One TFH Plaza
Third and Union Avenues
Neptune City, NJ 07753

This book has been published with the intent to provide accurate and authoritative information in regard to the subject matter within. While every precaution has been taken in preparation of this book, the publisher and author assume no responsibility for errors or omissions. Neither is any liability assumed for damages resulting from the use of the information herein.

ISBN 0-7938-0261-X

www.tfh.com

Distributed by T.F.H. Publications, Inc.
Neptune City, NJ

Contents

Many reptile keepers have fallen for the Bearded Dragon's endearing face and alert glance.

THE GUIDE TO OWNING A BEARDED DRAGON

Introducing Bearded Dragons

The herp hobby has come a long way since the days of keeping Painted Turtles in fish bowls. A combination of new technologies specific to captive herpetoculture and the infusion of new species into the hobby have helped to make herp keeping the fastest growing sector of the pet industry.

The infusion of new species has led to the discovery that some of these species are completely unsuitable for keeping in captivity, but many have turned out to be highly adaptable to life among humans. One of these desirable species is the Inland Bearded Dragon, *Pogona vitticeps*. Within the last few years, the Bearded Dragon has become one of the most widely kept of all lizards. They are found in many pet shops, show up on most wholesalers lists, and cover the vendor tables at herp shows and swap meets.

A well cared for Bearded Dragon can live seven years or more. Consider this before buying one.

Bearded Dragons spend much of their time basking to keep their body temperature up in their preferred active range.

The opposite is seen in a distant cousin to the Bearded Dragon, the Frilled Dragon, *Chlamydosaurus kingi*. This lizard, which also hails from Australia, is seldom available. Pet stores rarely stock them, and only occasionally is this fascinating lizard offered for sale by wholesalers and reptile show vendors. When available, the price can prohibit purchase.

While these two lizards are rather different and not closely related, including them in one book makes a certain amount of sense. They come from the same area of the world, often occurring in similar habitats. Both are active, sun-loving climbers. Both perform convincing threat displays. Keeping these lizards requires similar husbandry practices. Because they are more widely kept and more thoroughly understood, Bearded Dragons form the major focus of this book. What little that is known about Frilled Dragons is presented in the last section.

Recently, Bearded Dragons have become a herpetocultural sensation. In only a few years, this species has gone from obscurity to huge popularity, becoming a widely kept lizard. Upon first glance, you might wonder why. They are not brightly colored, nor are they particularly odd of shape or size. They look like a typical lizard. Collectively Bearded Dragons have just about the best temperament of all lizards. They are docile, and many seem to enjoy being handled. Better yet, they are aware and responsive. Bearded Dragons attentively watch you move about the room, sometimes literally begging for food. And they can certainly eat. A Bearded Dragon can be a veritable bottomless pit. Additionally, when housed in small groups, a number of interesting social behaviors can be observed. Of all the lizards, perhaps the Bearded Dragon is the one most deserving of the term "pet."

TAXONOMY

The genus *Pogona* is situated in the family Agamidae, a large and widespread Old World lineage. The Agamidae is a varied group that comprises some of the most bizarre lizards in existence. From the Flying Dragons (genus *Draco*) to the otherworldly Moloch (*Moloch horridus*), this family is like a carnival side show in its assortment. There are many "normal" species, however, including water dragons (genus *Physignathus*) and uromastyx (genus *Uromastyx*). The Frilled Dragon resides in this family as well.

When looking at the bulk of the Agamid species, most are fairly unspecialized, having only minor differences in their adaptations. The Bearded Dragon is a very typical example of the family. Most agamids have large heads, powerful legs, and long (comparatively) tails. Most possess strong development of the claws for digging or climbing, as well as well-formed dentition for eating a wide range of foods. Many species possess attractive dorsal crests and dewlaps. Agamids occur in many color forms, but most are relatively somberly colored and patterned. Some have the capability of color change, usually having to do with body temperature regulation. Most rely on their strong eyesight for

The awesome threat display of the Frilled Dragon has made it a standard feature in nature documentaries and a coveted animal among reptile hobbyists.

feeding and for predator detection. For the most part, the species of the family Agamidae are egg layers, except for the genus *Cophotis* and some species of *Phrynocephalus.*

DESCRIPTION

The Bearded Dragon and its relatives in the genus *Pogona* are natives of Australia. They live in many different habitats, including woodlands, grasslands, and deserts. The generalized form of these dragons, along with their basic hardiness, has allowed them to succeed in these diverse habitats. The genus *Pogona* contains species that are of a terrestrial or semi-arboreal existence. They are heavy-bodied with large heads, a slightly dorsally flattened body structure, and scales that vary a lot in size, shape, and color.

Adult males will reach 2 feet (61 centimeters) while females tend to be several inches shorter. About half of the length is made up by the tail.

Despite being spiny-looking, Bearded Dragons are not prickly to the touch.

The Bearded Dragon originally came in as just another lizard import from abroad, just one more oddball to be added to the collections of scientists or specialist herp keepers. It was quickly found, however, that this species— when kept in appropriate conditions— thrived and endeared itself to its keeper. Living from five to twelve years in captivity, this species can become a fixture in the reptile room. This is on top of a cherub-like appearance and behavior that may be the most amusing of any herp species currently kept.

BEHAVIOR

The Bearded Dragon gets its name from the slim, pointy spines that adorn the throat and ear openings of this species. In fact, the throat spines are just a prop in the spectacle that takes place during mating and territorial displays. Both male and female Bearded Dragons, but especially males,

Few reptiles are quite as appealing as a baby Bearded Dragon. Expect the hatchlings to be more wary than the adults.

Bearded Dragons are known for their comical antics. They frequently will pile on top each other.

are capable of darkening and inflating the throat region somewhat to increase their overall size and impressiveness. Head bobbing will accompany this behavior to maximize the whole effect. Even during the off-season, males will use their head bobbing and throat extension abilities when crossing another Bearded Dragon to establish dominance and territorial control.

One of the most interesting behaviors that is observed in *P. vitticeps,* along with some of the other species of *Pogona*, is arm waving. For the uninformed observer of this activity it actually looks like Bearded Dragons are waving "hello" to each other. The lizard stands high on three legs and waves one of its arms in a circular fashion. It looks like the animal is doing a butterfly stroke in swimming, but with only one arm. The waving is done in a slow, deliberate style that can last for several moments.

Saying "hello" is not actually too far from the truth. By studying this behavior, it has been found that arm waving is used in two main ways. First, it is used in recognition of other individuals of the species. It seems that arm waving exclusively is used at far distances and then mixed with head bobbing at close range. The second use of arm waving is during the mating season when females use the display as a form of submission for mating and/or to avoid aggression from the males.

Choosing a Bearded Dragon from a group is not easy. Look for one that is healthy and tame.

Arm waving appears to be a less severe, antagonistic behavior pattern than head bobbing. Youngsters use arm waving when interacting with each other without any apparent aggression. It is also probably the start of territorial behavior in the young animals. This display drops off as the animals reach maturity and is used mainly by females and submissive males to avoid aggression.

Another interesting behavior, tail raising, is quite common in Bearded Dragons kept together. Tail raising is used by Dragons to signify a state of tension or alertness. Just as many snakes vibrate their tails, Bearded Dragons will keep their tails in a relatively straight raised position until the threat has passed. This display is seen most frequently in animals that are being kept together for the first time. It is also seen in animals kept in cramped conditions. The behavior has also been used as a prelude to the head bobbing/arm waving in pairs before mating.

The final behavior pattern of note is the hierarchy display that occurs among captive Dragons. It seems that Bearded Dragons tend to arrange themselves in order of dominance in an enclosure. The dominant male will usually pick an obviously prominent location in the enclosure (such as a tree branch or a mound of rocks) on which to bask. The next most dominant animal will take a position in a less advantageous spot somewhere else in the enclosure, and so on. In nature, Bearded Dragons space themselves out in their own territories so this particular behavior pattern usually does not appear.

The Bearded Dragon displays a truly fascinating collection of behavior patterns. Although one specimen will show these behaviors to a certain extent, only when kept in groups will this species really "act natural." Give them enough space, as crowded Dragons will come under stress quickly and won't show you a very natural activity level.

ACQUIRING SPECIMENS

It is up to the hobbyist to zero in on the best source for his/her prized Bearded Dragon. There are several choices: 1) well-informed pet stores that stock reptiles on a regular basis will usually have several specimens of Bearded Dragon that are for sale. A store of this type is extremely valuable, in that the owners or sales clerks will have first-hand experience in keeping these animals. And all the literature in the world can't beat experience itself. These are some of the people to talk to in getting great information on your Bearded Dragons. 2) The second avenue in acquiring Bearded Dragons is the reptile "wholesaler." These companies, which advertise in various pet magazines, stock many species of reptiles—and often Dragons are plentiful. 3) One of the best places to go is the various herp societies that exist throughout the country and

world. These groups hold regular meetings (including swap meets—an excellent place to find rare and exotic species), go on field trips, and can be a good source of information.

When purchasing a specimen it is wise to research your potential purchase beforehand. Buying a Bearded Dragon on a whim frequently will lead to an improperly cared for lizard. All of the necessary components for a properly set up enclosure for a Bearded Dragon usually cannot be found in raiding your herp "scrap pile." The housing requirements for such a lizard cannot be met without some prior preparation on the part of the potential owner—as you will see in the next chapter.

Once you have your lizards in your possession, it is up to you to acclimate them to their new world. The first step, before you even consider introducing them to their new home, is to have them checked by veterinarian. True, a visit to a vet is not cheap, but for those who have invested (and for some of these specimens it can truly be called an investment) in a Bearded Dragon it is very important to follow this step. Since virtually all Bearded Dragons in the US and Europe are captive-bred, your new pet should be parasite-free. However, it is important to treat any health problems early, especially when an animal is stressed by acclimation to a new environment. At this time, ailments will rapidly worsen.

Pogona vitticeps is the species most people mean when they say "Bearded Dragon," but the name can apply to the whole genus.

Species
Accounts

The genus *Pogona* currently comprises several species, all native to continental Australia. Up until only recently the genus has been known under the "umbrella" genus of *Amphibolurus*.

Amphibolurus still exists, but it comprises only a fraction of the species that it once held. There are currently three species labeled *Amphibolurus*. They all once were

Wild Bearded Dragons sometimes take on a yellowish or reddish coloration and blend in with the sand and rocks in their locality.

Pogona vitticeps generally range from 7 to 8 inches in length. They are the most common member of *Pogona* found in the reptile hobby.

placed together with the species of the genus *Pogona*, but scientists who have studied these species in depth have concluded that there is enough difference to warrant separate generic placement.

Throughout Australia, from east to west, north to south, the species of *Pogona* inhabit several different climatic regions. They are opportunistic feeders, and all are quite similar in form and habits. In fact, it usually takes a trained eye to separate the species, due to only minor differences in body spines, skeletal make-up, and color patterning. So with this in mind, let's take a closer look at the species of the genus *Pogona*.

Pogona barbata (Cuvier, 1829)
Coastal Bearded Dragon

Length: 10 inches (snout to vent length)

Distribution: Ranges over the eastern and southeastern portions of Australia.

Habitat: A semi-arboreal species, seen mostly in woodlands or coastal scrublands. It is quite common near residential areas.

Description: The "other" species of Bearded Dragon that occasionally shows up for sale. It seems to be more common in European collections than in American ones. Differentiating between this species and *P. vitticeps* is fairly difficult. Some hints are that it grows to about 10 inches (snout-vent length), with a tail about 130% of the snout-vent length. This lizard is longer but slimmer than *P. vitticeps*.

P. barbata, for all intents and purposes, has identical needs as the "real" Bearded Dragon, *P. vitticeps*. Temperatures can be slightly cooler, but this is not a major issue. Housing and feeding requirements are exactly the same as *P. vitticeps*.

Pogona microlepidota (Glauert, 1952) Drysdale River Bearded Dragon

Length: 5 inches (snout to vent length)

Distribution: Native only to a portion of northwest Australia—Drysdale River, Western Australia

Habitat: Open woodland to scrubland, always near bushes, fallen trees, etc.

Description: This species is quite reminiscent of many New World species of swifts—it is fast, slender, and small. It also takes a mainly insectivorous diet, although like the other species of *Pogona*, it is opportunistic and will eat other small invertebrates as well as some flowers or other soft vegetation. They are rarely encountered in nature and the chances of them being legally imported from their isolated locality is slim. Still, it is nice to know they exist.

Specialist breeders occasionally produce hybrids between *Pogona vitticeps* and the undescribed *Pogona* "rankini", or Rankin's Dragon.

Pogona minima (Loveridge, 1933)
Western Bearded Dragon

Length: 6-7 inches (snout to vent length)

Distribution: Western and southwestern portion of Western Australia

Habitat: Mostly open scrubland and grassland

Description: A small and slender member of the genus, *P. minima* is rarely seen outside of Australia. This species is often confused with *P. minor*, even by those experienced with this genus. *P. minima* possesses a nuchal row of spines located on both sides of the head, whereas *P. minor* does not. *P. minima* takes on a more generalized lizard structure and habits, as it is quite opportunistic in its diet and habitat. In this regard it is reminiscent of the semi-arboreal swifts of the New World.

Pogona minor (Sternfeld, 1919)
Dwarf Bearded Dragon

Length: 6-7 inches (snout to vent length)

Distribution: Central Australia, west through Western Australia to the coast.

Habitat: A wide-ranging lizard, occupying grasslands, scrub forests, and open woodlands.

The Jacky Lizard, *Amphibolurus muricatus*, and the other members of its genus are closely related to *Pogona*.

With an expanded black "beard" and gaping yellow mouth, a Coastal Bearded Dragon, *Pogona barbata*, tries to ward off rivals and predators.

Description: A similar species to *P. minima*, in that it is quite generalized in its feeding and habitat requirements. It is also quite similar to *P. barbata*, although it possesses a more slender build and is quite a bit smaller.

This lizard is infrequently seen, although it is common in many parts of its range. Its diet consists of insects and other assorted invertebrates, along with some flowers.

Pogona mitchelli (Badham, 1976) Mitchell's Bearded Dragon

Length: 5-6 inches (snout to vent length)

Distribution: Central Australia, west through Western Australia to the coast. Very similar in range to *P. minor*, although not as extensive and not found in the southern portions of *P. minor's* range.

Habitat: Open woodlands containing lots of fallen trees and other cover; scrublands.

Description: A smaller version of *P. minor*, although having contiguous, conical spines in the spinous rows of the head. Another rarely seen species that is quite swift-like in movement and habits. It takes a diet similar to *P. minor* or *P. minima* and should do well in a semi-desert style enclosure. As with the other species of *Pogona*, keep this species in

The Coastal Bearded Dragon, *Pogona barbata*, is not common in American collections, although a few specialists are breeding them.

a roomy cage (very roomy, if you plan on keeping more than one together) with some branches for climbing.

Pogona nullarbor (Badham, 1976)
Banded Bearded Dragon

Length: 5-6 inches (snout to vent length)

Distribution: Restricted to the Nullarbor Plain in South and Western Australia.

Habitat: *P. nullarbor* is an adaptable species that is found in a semi-isolated area of southern Australia. In this range it occurs in eucalyptus forests and various scrublands, as well as open areas of coastal dunes.

Description: Quite similar to *P. barbata* and *microlepidota*, except for its obvious banding. In fact, this species is the most strongly patterned species in the genus *Pogona*. The whitish banding occurs across the back, starting at the neck and continuing well into the tail.

This is another of the rarely, if ever, imported species of *Pogona*. If, however, this species ever makes it to the hobby in any great numbers, it should become established relatively quickly. The small size, whitish banding, and personable behavior should help make it popular with hobbyists.

Pogona vitticeps (Ahl, 1926)
Inland Bearded Dragon, Central Bearded Dragon

Length: 7-8 inches (snout to vent length)

Although in completely different families, Bearded Dragons bear quite a resemblance to the New World swifts, genus *Sceloporus*.

THE GUIDE TO OWNING A BEARDED DRAGON

Pogona vitticeps occupies a wide range of habitat in the wild, from desert to forest, and is often found around human dwellings basking on picnic tables and fences.

The Western Bearded Dragon, *Pogona minima*, is a small species that is unavailable to reptile hobbyists.

Distribution: Eastern, central Australia, reaching the coast of southern Australia.

Habitat: This wide-ranging species occurs in a variety of environments, from forests to semi-arid scrubland and desert regions. It occurs in many inhabited regions where they are commonly seen on fenceposts, picnic tables, and such.

Description: The most heavy-bodied of the *Pogona* genus, this is the species common to the hobby. It is large, becomes quite docile, and has been bred in several color varieties including red and banded specimens. Captive specimens are known to grow much larger than wild specimens, probably because of the enriched diets that can be provided in captivity.

Housing

When housing Bearded Dragons, it is very important to remember a few things. First, Dragons are very active lizards. They tend to be curious and will investigate their environment thoroughly and regularly once acclimated. They need to be able to roam about, otherwise obesity

Young Bearded Dragons have similar housing requirements to the adults, including the need for climbing, hiding, and basking areas.

Although it makes a nice picture, young Bearded Dragons should not be housed with adults who will out-compete them for food and basking sites.

could result from the forced inactivity.

Second, Bearded Dragons are very territorial, being quite bent on finding themselves their own piece of land. Bearded Dragons will come under stress rapidly if kept in crowded conditions with conspecifics larger than themselves. They will ignore food, frequently hide, and slowly waste away until their untimely demise.

Bearded Dragons do not necessarily need to have their native habitat reconstructed to the "T." They do, however, need to have certain aspects of their environment replicated in captivity. Failure to do this will inevitably lead to a sorry ending. So with these thoughts in mind, we will be able to successfully house Bearded Dragons.

You must decide just what it is exactly that you want to do with Bearded Dragons. Do you want just one as a pet? Do you want to have two or three animals in the same enclosure? Or do you have breeding on your mind? Once you decide on what particular Bearded Dragon setup you want to go with, you can put the enclosure together.

A group of hatchling Bearded Dragons can be housed on newspaper which is very cheap and easy to change.

All Bearded Dragons like to climb and will suffer from stress if the keeper does not provide branches and/or rocks to climb on.

SPACE, NUMBERS, AND SIZE

It is probably best to start out with just one juvenile specimen if you are new to Bearded Dragons. A hatchling is more delicate, and adults don't give the keeper the satisfaction obtained by watching them grow. However, if you intend to breed them, start with a pair of animals that is mature but still young.

Housing each different size of lizard has its own problems. Hatchling and juvenile Bearded Dragons are in a stage where they are growing quickly. They have voracious appetites and will often mistake each other for food. We have seen too many examples of these lizards with missing toes, tail tips, etc. Adults, on the other hand, ignore each other as possible food items, but become quite territorial and look to establish a niche for themselves.

What we are saying here is that you will want to give enough space for each individual lizard—whether or not they are housed together—to allow them to live comfortably and without any undue stress.

Young dragons can be kept together, provided there is ample space and food. However, they ideally should be housed individually as mentioned before. If given enough room, however, a small colony can be comfortably maintained in one enclosure. For 3-4"

Bearded Dragons are territorial. If you house more than one together, be sure you have an adequately-sized cage.

dragons allow an area approximately the size of a 10-gallon aquarium (20" x 10" x 12"). Hatchlings will do fine with less area per lizard; larger dragons will obviously need more room due to their aggressive behavior. The bare minimum size for an adult Bearded Dragon is a 40-gallon breeder aquarium (36"x18"x14"); for a pair, use at least a 100-gallon tank. Remember that these are active lizards.

It is always better to oversize an aquarium or cage for Bearded Dragons as their individual temperaments can vary quite widely. One juvenile in a 10-gallon aquarium is fine; four or five in a 40-gallon aquarium is good, and so on. Keep in mind that even groups kept in spacious terraria will be somewhat territorial and prone to fighting if inadequately fed.

Custom wooden cages can be used and are a good idea if you intend to house a colony of large adults. This is because the large aquarium needed to keep a colony is physically quite heavy and will be fairly expensive to purchase. A wooden cage will be cheaper to construct, although more difficult to keep clean due to the porous nature of wood. A non-toxic lacquer coating on the wood can make clean-ups easier.

Playground sand is an excellent substrate for Bearded Dragon enclosures. There are also brands designed for reptiles.

THE GUIDE TO OWNING A BEARDED DRAGON

Sand is a commonly used substrate for Bearded Dragons. Pet shops have a variety of substrates and cage accessories available.

Some pet stores and reptile specialty shops carry cages made from molded plastic; these often have sliding doors in the front or side. These tend to be expensive, but they are lightweight, durable, and easy to clean. They also hold heat well. If your local pet store does not stock these, talk to the personnel about ordering them.

SUBSTRATES

Now that you have an idea of the space requirements for Bearded Dragons you will need to furnish and equip the cage. First, a substrate will be needed. The best bottom covering for Bearded Dragons is playground sand or fine gravel. This is non-toxic, easily passes through a lizard's digestive tract if swallowed, simulates the natural habitat, and is easily and inexpensively replaced. A layer of about 2-3" should suffice and will need to be kept clean of waste on a regular basis to keep odor down. Check with a pet store to get advice on the available brands of substrate that are safe for reptiles.

There are also other substrates that are suitable. Aquarium gravels up to a size #3 are fine. They tend to collect detritus (and odor) and will need to be cleaned on a more regular basis to avoid a rather organic odor. They are washable and reusable, and come in a variety of colors and sizes. Be aware that the use of gravel may cause blockage of the lizard's intestines.

Another substrate that is fine for dragons is reptile carpeting (not artificial turf). Many pet stores carry this in one brand or another. It shows up waste very well (making it easier to determine when to clean the cage) and is easy to clean, which will lend itself to keeping a lizard in a healthy environment. It can be expensive, but it is reusable many times.

Many keepers use some form of bark or mulch. There are bark beddings specific for reptiles on the market. Most of them can be cleaned;

make sure you have extra to use while the old batch is drying out. Lastly, bedding made from recycled paper can also be used as long as it is the soft fibrous kind and claims to be safe for reptiles.

CAGE FURNISHINGS

After a suitable substrate has been selected, interior decor can be chosen to provide both cover for the lizards and a visually pleasing setup. For the breeder or one who wishes only to furnish the bare basics, the required equipment is as follows.

A hidebox will be necessary to afford the lizard with a sense of security, a retreat from other more dominant dragons in the same

When housing a group of hatchling Dragons, feeding, cleaning, and watering need to be done daily or more frequently.

THE GUIDE TO OWNING A BEARDED DRAGON

Bearded Dragons will hold their mouths open when they get too hot. This helps them cool down.

Branches and rocks must be securely fixed in place to prevent them from falling and injuring your Bearded Dragons.

enclosure, and possibly a place to deposit eggs. If more than one specimen will be kept per enclosure, a hidebox should be provided for each animal, in separate corners of the enclosure if possible. Hideboxes can be made of wood or formed by sturdy rocks, or shoeboxes can be used (the plastic types are the best as they are sturdy and easy to clean). Entry and exit holes should be made, without any sharp edges. The box must be big enough to allow the lizard to turn around inside the box completely and easily.

Another necessary piece of equipment is the water bowl. Although native to brushland and semi-desert regions, Bearded Dragons need a steady supply of clean drinking water. They also are fond of soaking (and defecating) in water, so a water bowl large enough to accommodate your lizard's body should be used. The bowl should be ruggedly made, preferably out of thick, molded plastic or ceramic. Ideally the bowl should be large enough to be able to handle the size of the lizard, as well as have enough weight to be able to withstand attempts at overturning the bowl by the lizard.

Be careful that humidity levels stay very low. High humidity can cause respiratory and skin ailments. Some keepers offer their Dragons water for only an hour or two each day, removing the bowl after this period. Hatchlings seem to drink more than adults.

Your Bearded Dragon's cage should be well-maintained and kept clean. Rocks and branches add to the Dragon's home and give it places to explore.

Some keepers use aspen or pine shavings for a substrate. These are easy to clean and fairly inexpensive.

As semi-arboreal animals, Bearded Dragons must have some branches or rockwork that they can use for exercising and territorial acquisition. Each Dragon should have its own area of branches or rocks in order to keep territorial run-ins to a minimum. A good idea to keep in mind is that, when housing more than one Bearded Dragon, the more vertical space that can be utilized by the lizards the less chance there is of a scuffle. Less stress equals healthier animals.

You will need a securely fitting cover to keep your specimens where they belong. The metal mesh types available at your local pet store are inexpensive, sturdy, and allow excellent ventilation. A medium grade mesh is perfect. This type of cover will easily support a light hood. Alternately, you can construct your own cover from chicken wire incorporated into a wooden frame.

LIGHTING AND HEATING

Lighting the Bearded Dragon enclosure is not difficult if you understand what the lighting is needed for. First, lighting will be

In a large terrarium, cinder blocks and ceramic tiles can be used for climbing and hiding materials. These Dragons have taken to them nicely.

Artificial plants contribute to the aesthetics of the terrarium and provide cover for the Dragons.

THE GUIDE TO OWNING A BEARDED DRAGON

Cattle watering troughs are used as housing by some keepers. Watch out for Dragons getting out and other pets getting in.

necessary to supply ultraviolet light to the lizards. This allows the Dragons to synthesize vitamin D3 in their tissues. It seems that without a steady supply of vitamin D3, Dragons are at risk of various ailments, mainly metabolic bone disease. The best source of ultraviolet radiation is the sun. Of course, allowing your Bearded Dragon to bask outdoors is unrealistic unless you live in a tropical or sub-tropical climate. A good substitute is full-spectrum fluorescent lighting. Plant bulbs are not suitable for reptiles. Several bulbs designed to provide the wavelengths of light that reptiles need have entered the market recently. These bulbs are available at many pet shops and some hardware stores. The best setup is to run one or two bulbs the length of the enclosure.

Lighting also provides heat. Incandescent lighting is the best at raising the cage temperature, but fluorescent lighting is still needed to provide UV light. At least one spotlight should be set up to allow a specific area of the tank to reach 90-100°F. The ambient air temperature in the cage should be 80-84°F. Make sure the spotlight is not placed directly in the tank, but safely housed above it. A reflector dome will focus the heat into the cage. Having a basking site for each Dragon in the enclosure is a good idea. A reliance on hot rocks or undertank heat pads will usually be inadequate.

Lighting should be left on for 12-14 hours per day; the ultraviolet lights can be turned off after about 8 hours, if desired. A smart idea is to rig the lighting to separate timers so that it will make things easier for you and also allow the lizards a more natural routine. Adjustments to the amount of light can be made to simulate seasonal changes if you have intentions of breeding Bearded Dragons.

At night, temperatures can drop to 65-75°F. Using a low wattage red heat bulb will maintain this temperature without disturbing the Dragon's day-night cycle. Ceramic heat emitters that give off heat but not light are also useful.

THE NATURALISTIC SETUP

The equipment listed above is necessary to the well-being of your lizards. However, if you are interested in setting up more than just the basics, this section is for you. Knowing the natural habitat of the Bearded Dragon, the only thing that you have to do now is incorporate those environmental conditions into a smaller version.

The same cage sizes can be used for a naturalistic enclosure as for a basic one. However, the bigger the enclosure, the easier it will be to make it appear more natural. Of course, the bigger the enclosure, the more expensive it will be. Start with a layer of sand, small-grained gravel, or a combination of both. About 3 or 4" should suffice. This will add quite a bit of weight to the overall setup, so make sure that you have a sturdy surface to place it on.

Rockwork should make up a good portion of the decorations. Many types of rock can be employed here. Again,

If you house a colony of Bearded Dragons, be sure that you provide plenty of room for exercise and several nest boxes. This will keep territorial squabbling to a minimum.

THE GUIDE TO OWNING A BEARDED DRAGON

Bearded Dragons can become stressed if their living conditions are too crowded or are unclean. Be sure to keep your Beardie's content.

keep in mind some types can be quite dense and heavy. A good choice for decorating is lava or tufa rock. Both are quite pretty, lightweight, and easily acquired from pet stores and garden centers. They can be stacked to form outcroppings or strewn throughout the tank to simulate a desert "wasteland."

The last piece of decoration that you may want to use is branchwork. You can purchase it at pet stores or collect your own. Make sure that pieces that you collect on your own are insect-free. Soak the branches in a weak solution of bleach for several hours, then make sure to rinse them well and dry them before placing them in the enclosure.

When laying out your design you will want to try and maximize the amount of territories that are present. This will quickly become important when you have several young Dragons that are becoming sexually mature. Without any territory delineation, young Dragons will constantly be fighting and injuring themselves. It may be necessary to set up more than one water bowl and more than one feeding dish to allow all the lizards to feed. Likewise, multiple hiding places and basking sites should be used (one for each animal) to keep stress down.

The naturalistic arrangement not only will make an impressive addition to any room, but will also keep stress to a minimum between the Bearded Dragons.

Bearded Dragons are very enthusiastic eaters, which is part of the fun of keeping them.

Feeding

Once the housing for your Bearded Dragons is complete, a proper nutrition program is in order. In the natural habitat, Bearded Dragons are opportunistic omnivores, meaning they will take a wide selection of animal and vegetable fare. Hatchlings and juveniles take a greater amount

Do not feed any lizards more crickets than they can eat at once as hungry crickets have been known to attack lizards.

Water must be changed frequently because Bearded Dragons will kick pieces of substrate in the bowl or even defecate in it.

of animal matter (insects, other arthropods, small vertebrates, anything that fits in their mouths). Adults eat similar but larger things and seem to more eagerly eat vegetation than the younger lizards.

The healthy Bearded Dragon is an active, foraging lizard. It will eat virtually anything that it thinks is edible. This is a great feature of this lizard. However, it can give the keeper a false sense of security. A Dragon will be all too happy to eat every mealworm and piece of iceberg lettuce that you throw into the cage. This is, of course, not a good idea. Mealworms, when used in con-

junction with a variety of other food items, can make an excellent addition to a Bearded Dragon's diet. However, mealworms do not supply all the lizard's nutritional needs. Iceberg lettuce has virtually no value at all and should not be used. It is up to you to ignore, in a sense, the fact that your lizard relishes foods that are limited in their nutritive value and concentrate on providing a complete diet for your charges.

WHAT TO FEED

Insects make up most of the proper diet for a Bearded Dragon. Crickets, mealworms (regular and king), waxworms, and field-caught bugs should all be used. Insects at pet stores usually do not have access to high quality foods and are often depleted of nutrients. It is, therefore, important that insects purchased at pet stores be fed a nutritious diet before feeding them to your lizards. This process of feeding the insects to make them more nutritious is called gut-loading. Gut-loading works well with crickets and mealworms, but waxworms eat a specialized diet and cannot be gut-loaded. You should place crickets and mealworms in separate, escape-proof, well-ventilated enclosures containing oatmeal, wheat bran, flake fish food, and/or dry dog food mixed with calcium and vitamin supplements. Add some pieces of vegetables to provide some nutrients and moisture. By the next day they will be ready to feed to your lizards. Gut-loading is a significant factor in how some species of lizard do over the long haul. Bearded Dragons, especially young or sick specimens, will benefit greatly. It is certainly worth the extra time needed to prepare the insects, as opposed to just dumping the insects into the cage.

Never feed herps more crickets than they will eat at once. Crickets left in a cage will become hungry and possibly attempt to dine on your animal. This is not a joke; crickets can injure or even kill a reptile, especially a hatchling. The same applies to mealworms. Feed mealworms to your lizards in a shallow bowl to prevent them from escaping into the cage and causing havoc later.

Locusts and grasshoppers are good to include in the diet of adult Bearded Dragons.

Although many wild plants are fine for Dragons, the spines on the flower-heads of this species make it a dangerous choice.

Other animal matter can also be present in the diet of a Bearded Dragon. Some will eagerly devour canned dog or cat food. This is a healthy addition to the diet if used sparingly, say no more than a tablespoon once a week for an adult (less for young).

Most Dragons will eat small mice eagerly. These are too high in fat to make a good staple food, but mice are excellent sources of protein, calcium, and other nutrients. They make a good occasional treat.

Vegetable matter should make up a substantial portion of a Bearded Dragon's diet: 10-25% for hatchlings and young, 30-50% for an adult (about two years old). A wide variety of vegetables can be offered. Basically, the whole produce department of your local grocery store is useful. You don't need to use six or eight types at every feeding; just make sure to use at least two or three types and rotate others in on a regular basis. Some of the best vegetables and fruits to use are romaine lettuce, mustard and collard greens, turnip tops, dandelion leaves and flowers, parsley, squashes, raspberries, and grated carrots.

All vegetables should be chopped or grated into bite-size pieces. Do not allow vegetables to sit in the cage for longer than a day; the warm environment will spoil them. Most Bearded Dragons prefer insects to vegetables, so you may want to feed them the vegetation first.

VITAMINS

To make sure that your Dragons are getting all the vitamins and minerals they need, you will need to enhance the regular diet with a commercial vitamin supplement. There are several reptile vitamin and mineral supplements available. Use one that has a wide variety of vitamins and minerals, is high in calcium, and is low in phosphorus. The use of a separate calcium supplement might be wise, particularly for rapidly growing young and breeding females. Check with your pet store to see what is available.

A plate of grated carrots and kale forms today's serving of vegetables. Feed Bearded Dragons a wide range of vegetables, flowers, and fruits.

It is important to follow the directions on the package or (even better) to consult a veterinarian about the dosage. Although not a common problem, captive reptiles can be over-fed vitamins, which causes all manner of serious ailments as the vitamins reach toxic levels in the body.

The best route to take is to choose between either supplementing the vegetables or the insects. Vitamins can be lightly sprinkled over the fruits and vegetables, or, if your Bearded Dragon is eating insects much better than vegetables, you may want to vitamin dust the crickets. The procedure is simple. Find yourself a small plastic bag. Add a small amount (about 1/2 teaspoon) of vitamin powder. Add the crickets to the bag. Close the bag and lightly shake. The

Mealworms add some variety to the diet of Bearded Dragons but should not be fed too often.

crickets will appear whitish or light gray in color. They can now be fed to your lizards. Remember, use vitamins on a regular basis but not too often, and if you have any questions at all as to dosage or frequency, check with a vet or experienced herp dealer.

HATCHLING DIET

If you purchase a hatchling (up to three months old) or produce hatchlings, you must know how to feed them during this critical period. Young Dragons grow rapidly and need lots of nutritious food. Also, if housing a group of young together, keeping them well fed will help prevent them from picking on each other.

Before discussing amounts of food, we must discuss size of food. All food for baby Bearded Dragons should be smaller than their head. This means you will need a ready supply of tiny crickets, fruitflies, houseflies, and waxworms. Pet stores can obtain 2-3-week old crickets for you, but you may have to order in large quantities. **Do not** feed mealworms to baby Bearded Dragons! Mealworms are too large and hard to digest for the young. Eating mealworms while this young can result in paralysis or death.

Hatchling Bearded Dragons should be offered insects two or three times daily. Make sure each individual gets a couple. If any of them are getting

Most Bearded Dragons quickly take to hand-feeding but be careful that you don't get bitten accidentally.

Most keepers use crickets as the base diet for Bearded Dragons. Make sure they are not too big for hatchlings.

out-competed for food, set them up in a separate enclosure. Vegetables should be offered two or three times each week. Chop the vegetables into bite-sized pieces. During this period of a Dragon's life, give vitamins with one feeding each day.

JUVENILE DIET

Juveniles (four months to about 18 months) are a little easier to feed than hatchlings, because they are larger, are growing a little less rapidly, and have somewhat larger reserves of fat on their bodies. As the Dragon grows, the size of its food can grow as well, still keeping all foods smaller than the animal's head. Small mealworms, preferably just-molted (soft and white), can now be added to the diet. An occasional pinky or fuzzy mouse will probably be relished by the Dragon now, as well.

Juveniles should be fed insects once a day. Healthy juveniles can skip a feeding every so often with no ill effects. Vegetables should be fed three times a week or so; vitamins also can be given this often.

ADULT DIET

Adults rarely have any problems with the size of their prey insects, and even small adult mice can be fed to them with no concern. Feed adults once a day or every other day. A skipped feeding now and again will cause no harm. Vegetables should be offered at every other feeding. Use vitamins once or twice each week. Bearded Dragons commonly become obese, so watch your pet's weight once it becomes an adult.

Breeding

The Bearded Dragon is not a particularly difficult species to breed. In fact, it is now one of the most frequently captive-bred lizards, probably second only to the Leopard Gecko, *Eublepharis macularius.* Many keepers breed Dragons on a commercial or individual scale. Several color varieties are produced, including red-phase, gold head, and banded.

Several components are important in the breeding of Bearded Dragons. First, you must have a pair of sexually mature animals. Telling the sexes of Bearded Dragons apart is not always easy. Until they are mature, it is quite easy to confuse the sexes. In adults, behavior is a fairly reliable indicator. Males will display their beard, bob their heads, and defend territory. Adult males rarely display arm-waving behavior. There are physical differences as well: males will have

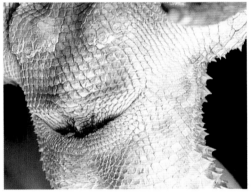

Above: Male Bearded Dragons usually have enlarged scales before the vent, a large vent opening, and hemipenal bulges after the vent.

Below: Females, in contrast, have a smaller vent opening and do not have enlarged scales or hemipenal bulges.

This large female is laying her eggs in a container of moist sand. Lack of a nesting area can cause health problems for both the eggs and the mother.

THE GUIDE TO OWNING A BEARDED DRAGON

Hatchlings grow quickly. Note the size difference between these two hatchlings. The Beardie on the left is approximately 2 months old, the one on the right is 4 months old.

very prominent femoral and preanal pores, males are larger, males have larger and more blocky heads. If in doubt, consult your veterinarian or a pet shop employee.

Age is an important factor. Bearded Dragons come into sexual maturity during their second year and remain prolific through their fifth or sixth year. After this, Bearded Dragons tend to decline in their reproductive success rates. Make sure the pair you want to breed are between two and five years old. Next, the Dragons that you want to breed must be conditioned, be put "in the mood." Several months before

breeding, make sure the pair is in good health. Feed them well, but make sure they are not obese.

HIBERNATION

Most reptiles in the wild are very seasonal in their breeding efforts, and Bearded Dragons are no exception. As winter comes, it cools down, there is less light, and the abundance of food wanes. Bearded Dragons react to this by going into a semi-hibernation state. Hibernation triggers the development of the reproductive cells and sets the stage for the production of young. So, to elicit breeding, a cool-down period must be given. If the health of the animals is in any way questionable, do not put them through the stress of hibernation; it may cause their death.

Over the period of a few weeks, cool down the enclosure and reduce the duration of lighting. You are aiming for a daytime temperature of 75-80°F, with the nighttime temperature at 60-70°F. Lighting should be reduced to 8-10 hours per day. Again, make these changes gradually. During this time period, the Dragons will be less active and may eat very little.

Hibernation should last 8-12 weeks. Gradually raise the temperature back up to normal and increase the photoperiod. Feed the pair as much as they will eat. Adding some extra calcium to the female's food may be wise. You may observe mating behavior, but you may not as it is over quickly. You will observe more occurrences of head-bobbing and arm-waving. Be sure that the male is not getting too aggressive. If the female is

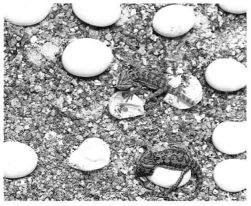
Vermiculite is the most widely used incubation media for reptiles. It is available at pet and garden stores.

not eating, has bites or cuts, or seems to be intimidated by the male, separate the pair for a week or so. Some small bites on the back of the female's neck are normal during mating, and, as long as they are not severe or infected, you shouldn't worry about them.

NESTING AND LAYING

Keep a close eye on the female. In a month or two, she will get noticeably plump, and you may actually be able to see the outline of eggs through her abdomen. She will start digging and scratching at the substrate. If you haven't already put a nesting box in the enclosure, now is the time.

Different keepers use different nesting boxes and substrates. Whatever box you use, it should be longer than the female and allow at least 5 inches of substrate. A roof is not necessary. Cactus soil in a mid-size cat-litter pan works well. Vermiculite is also a good choice. Keep the substrate damp, but not wet.

When the time comes, the female will dig a burrow (hopefully in the box) and lay 10-25 eggs. She will sit completely in her burrow, usually with just the tip of her snout sticking out. When she is done, she will cover the eggs up, often so well the nest box will look virtually undisturbed. She will be noticeably lighter and flabby-looking. Feed her well with calcium-rich foods for she can produce up to four more clutches this year at roughly one-month intervals!

INCUBATION

For the greatest level of success, you should remove the eggs (do not turn them over) and put them in an incubator. You will need to make or buy an incubator at least a week before the eggs are laid, so that you can obtain a reliably steady temperature. Incubators are fairly simple to make. Two clean clay bricks should be placed in a 10-gallon tank or styrofoam cooler. Fill the tank with enough water to cover a submersible aquarium heater placed in the bottom. The temperature needs to be 83-85°F. A digital thermometer with a probe will assist you greatly in monitoring the temperature. A plastic container (a cheap food storage container is fine) containing 2 inches of moistened vermiculite is set on the bricks. The eggs should then be gently half-buried into the vermiculite. Keep the vermiculite moistened, but do not wet the eggs. A cover should then be placed over the tank to keep the air temperature steady. Make sure the cover allows for some air circulation, otherwise the lack of oxygen will kill the eggs. A piece of plexiglass with a bunch of holes drilled into it should do the trick. Watch the eggs for the next day

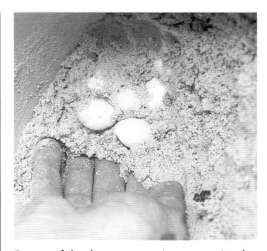

Be careful when uncovering eggs in the laying box. Turning them over can kill the embryos.

or so to make sure they don't shine from moisture condensation—this is a sign they are too wet. Also check to see that the eggs don't deflate—this is sign they are too dry. Discard any eggs that are deflated, oozing, or moldy as soon as you notice them.

If all goes well, the eggs will hatch in 8-11 weeks. Usually all the eggs will hatch in a 24-hour period. Do not try to assist the babies in hatching; you will probably kill them. Put the new hatchlings in a basic cage setup, individually if possible. They will usually not feed for 1-3 days, as they are still absorbing their yolks. You will need plenty of small insects to feed them once they start eating. A new generation of Bearded Dragons has arrived!

Disease and First Aid

All herp keepers should have a base of knowledge about reptile disease. Because of the fact that reptiles can hide disease until they are too far gone to attempt reversing the effects, it is vital to have a working understanding of spotting, identifying, and (possibly) treating diseases of your reptiles. Some of the more common diseases can be successfully treated in your own home; others will need veterinary assistance. However, you should realize that once a disease is apparent there may be nothing you can do.

PARASITES

Because most of the Bearded Dragons in the pet trade are captive-bred, the keeper seldom encounters parasites. If parasites are present, they usually have spread from another reptile in the collection. There are two major types of parasites: ectoparasites (external) and endoparasites (internal).

Ectoparasites usually take the form of ticks or mites and are easily treatable. Ticks can be as large as 1/4" long, but once attached and sucking blood can bloat up to the size of a grape. They can fasten themselves to virtually any body part of a lizard and hold on with their piercing mouthparts. There are several different methods to remove ticks. First, the tick can be smeared with petroleum jelly (which will cut off the oxygen supply to the parasite), at which point the tick will remove itself from the host in an attempt to breathe and can then be taken away for disposal. The second way to remove a tick is to dab some rubbing alcohol on the tick. This will cause the tick to relax its mouthparts, and then it can be gently pulled out with tweezers. Many pet stores carry commercial tick removers designed for reptiles. Follow the instructions on the package and get the advice of store personnel.

Mites are treated in a different manner. They usually are found only after they have multiplied into considerable numbers, which can occur very quickly. They congregate in the crevices of a lizard's body. Armpits, ear openings, and vent openings are common areas. The mites that affect herps are grayish in color and are very small (about the size of a grain of salt). Mites that have fed on blood will turn a scarlet or brownish color. Often, mites are detected only by finding them dead in a water bowl or by seeing their feces (whitish dust) between the scales of the infected animal. If one animal in a terrarium has mites, it is best to treat all the animals in the same terrarium as infected.

Mites can be difficult to get rid of. No method is guaranteed, and it is likely that you will need to repeat treatments. While treating the lizards, thoroughly clean the cage: replace the old substrate with new, soak all cage furnishings in bleach for at least an hour, wash the cage itself with bleach and let it sit for at least an hour, rinse and dry the cage furnishings before returning the lizard to the terrarium. It may be worth your while to use a cheap and easily replaceable substrate (newspaper or aspen bedding) while battling mites, as you may have to replace the substrate a few times. When you are positive the mites are gone, you can use your preferred substrate once again.

We recommend isolating parasitized individuals in a room that contains no other reptiles. Also, thoroughly wash your hands after handling a mite-ridden animal. These steps will prevent the spread of mites to your other herps.

Several methods to treat the lizard can be used. First, as with ticks, many pet stores carry reptile mite removers. Follow the directions exactly; overdosing could kill your lizard. Second, you can use a pest strip that has the active ingredient dichlorovinyl dimethyl diphosphate (often called dichlorvos). Put a half-inch piece of the strip in a small container. The container should be perforated to allow the vapors to escape but not so open that the lizard can touch it; salt shakers and small cardboard boxes should work. Place this container in the terrarium with the lizard. It is important to remover the water bowl during this treatment. Leave this in the terrarium for two days; remove it and replace the water bowl for three days. Repeat this process for 15 days (three treatments). All the mites should be gone, but you should keep checking for them for a few weeks before assuming your Dragon is mite-free.

If you don't like to use harsh chemicals, you can try washing the

Young Dragons will overheat and dehydrate much faster than adults. Always keep a thermometer in your terrarium.

mites off of your Dragon. Hold the lizard under a gently flowing faucet; obviously use warm water. Scrub the lizard gently with your fingers. The cage will need to be scrubbed out with a bleach solution, also. This method is the least reliable, and you will need to repeat it several times.

Endoparasites occur less frequently but are more serious. They can take the forms of tapeworms, round-worms, amoebic infections, and so on. Accurate identification is impossible without taking a fresh stool sample to a veterinarian. Some warning signs are lack of appetite, vomiting, sluggishness, sunken eyes, thinness, lack of muscletone, and watery waste matter. These symptoms are the same as for some bacterial infections, so treatment should be sought from a professional immediately.

OTHER INFECTIONS

Bacterial and fungal diseases are not at all common in healthy Bearded Dragons. A healthy specimen will keep infection to a minimum. However, any lizard kept in an environment that is dirty or otherwise stressful can come down with an illness. These maladies can be fatal if not treated and should always be handled by a vet. Symptoms of digestive tract infections are the same as for endoparasites, plus a possibility of blood in the feces. The symptoms of respiratory infections include nasal discharge, crusty matter around the nostrils and/or eyes, inactivity, and, in serious cases, open-mouth breathing and gasping.

MOUTH ROT

One infection that deserves special mention is mouth rot. As the name implies, this is a nasty infection of the

THE GUIDE TO OWNING A BEARDED DRAGON

gums and mouth lining, usually caused by bacteria and fungus entering a small wound. In severe cases it can infect the jawbones. The symptoms are swelling of the gums and/or jaw, refusal to eat, blood on the inside of the mouth, and a thick cheesy material in the mouth. Mouth rot can be very serious, and vet care is needed quickly. Until you can get to a vet, use a cotton swab to clean out the infected area. The swab should be dipped in peroxide or a povidone iodine solution or a mixture of the two.

SUPPORTIVE THERAPY

Any infections should be tended to by a reptile veterinarian. Yet, the keeper can do certain things to help the animal recover. The first is to keep the temperature high. The hot end of the cage should reach 100-105°F, with the cooler end around 80°F. Do not reduce the temperature at night while the animal is sick.

The second is to slightly raise the humidity, especially if the animal is not eating or drinking. A light misting once a day should be adequate. The third is to increase the amount of vitamins and minerals in the diet. Adding vitamins to one additional feeding per week is probably good.

If your Bearded Dragon goes off food during its illness, do not panic unless it doesn't eat for three or four days or weight-loss is noted. At this point, if you have not taken it to a vet, do so. Your vet can give you advice on force-feeding if he or she feels it is necessary. While the lizard is not eating, try to coax it to drink a little of a fruit-flavored sports drink. These are high in carbohydrates and electrolytes and are easily absorbed by the digestive tract.

SALMONELLA

Recently there has been a growing concern over reptile-associated salmonellosis. Most reptiles are thought to carry Salmonella and other bacteria that are harmless to their hosts most of the time. In humans, these bacteria are not so harmless. Salmonellosis in humans causes gastric distress, diarrhea, and vomiting. In a healthy adult, it is rarely serious. In children, the elderly, and immunocompromised individuals, it can be life-threatening.

However, despite the alarmists, the transmission of infections from reptile to human is infrequent and almost totally preventable. To prevent a bout of salmonellosis, strict hygiene regiments must be followed. Always wash your hands with soap and hot water after handling your Bearded Dragon or any items from its cage. Any areas the lizard or cage furnishings have come in contact with should be cleaned with a disinfectant. Bearded Dragons and their cage furnishings should never be placed on a surface that is used for food preparation (e.g., kitchen tables and counters). If a sink or bathtub is used to clean the cage or furnishings, wash it out with a strong bleach solution.

Lastly, children must be closely supervised when handling reptiles. They must not put the lizard, any cage items, or their own hands in their mouths. If children are allowed to handle your reptiles, it is your responsibility to prevent what could be a very serious incident.

INJURIES AND FIRST AID

Most other problems encountered in Bearded Dragons are injuries of one form or another. Most will not be serious. Prevention is better than treatment. Most injuries can be prevented by keeping sharp or pointed decorations out of the cage, making sure all branches and rocks are stable, only handling the lizard in a secure environment, and not allowing other household pets contact with the Bearded Dragons. If an injury does result, its size and severity will determine your course of action.

Suspected fractures must always be taken to a vet. Only treatment by a vet can prevent malformation of the limb during healing. Also, fractures are frequently accompanied by shock, so prompt vet care is very important.

Small cuts and abrasions usually can be treated by the keeper, provided they are not deep or bleeding heavily. Clean the wound with peroxide or povidone iodine (available at many drug stores). Smearing a little bit of antibiotic ointment on the wound is also a good idea. Check the appearance of the injury, clean it, and dab some new antibiotic ointment on it daily. If there are any signs of infection, get veterinary treatment as soon as you can. If the wound occurred because of fighting between tankmates, you should separate the individuals involved.

Untreated wounds, even tiny ones, can become abscesses. They will appear as round lumps under the skin. All abscesses require veterinary care. The vet will incise, drain, clean, and suture the injury. He or she will also prescribe antibiotics to combat reinfection and septicemia.

Unfortunately, burns are one of the most frequently seen injuries in reptiles. Burns mainly occur because an animal was allowed to get too close to a heatlamp or other heating device. Think prevention. It is best to seek veterinary care for any burn, even minor ones. Since burns are prone to infection, keep them very clean and use an antibiotic ointment. You can rub some fresh aloe vera juice on the burn to speed healing.

The Frilled Dragon

For many hobbyists, our fascination with herps began with the dinosaurs. As children we collected plastic dinosaur replicas and devoured any available books on the subject. At some point, we discovered the living dinosaurs, reptiles, and so began our life-long hobby. If you are one of us, then you, too, are probably fascinated with the Frilled Dragon, *Chlamydosaurus kingi*. Not many other herps so vividly recall the

Given enough space and adequate temperatures, Frilled Dragons will thrive in captivity.

terrible lizards that captured our imaginations so long ago. The frill for which they are named flares up around the neck like a shield, giving them the appearance of a miniature dinosaur. If that wasn't enough, like their extinct cousins, Frilled Dragons will run on two legs! The Frilled Dragon truly seems to be a Cretaceous relic.

For many reasons Frilled Dragons are not common in the hobby. One of these is that most of its natural range is in Australia, which does not export its fauna. Another is that they are not frequently bred by hobbyists or commercial dealers. These first two reasons produce a third reason: price. Frilled Dragons typically run $500 or more per lizard. Still, many herpers dream of owning their own *Chlamydosaurus*.

A Frilled's body can be up to 10" (25 cm.) long with the tail up to double this length. So, although Frilled's can be fairly large lizards, two-thirds of their length is their tail. The frill itself can measure up to 1' (30 cm.) accross. These lizards vary quite a bit in color, from olive through grayish brown to black. There is often light banding on the tail and speckles or spots on the flanks. The frills also show great variety; the color can be yellow, black, or any shade in between. Mottling and/or patching of orange often occurs on the throat and the frill.

As was stated, these lizards are found in Australia; additionally they occur in New Guinea. Their habitat is semi-arid open scrub forest. They are very agile and climb well, feeding on the ground and in the trees. They are opportunistic carnivores, hunting any small moving target. With great speed, powerful jaws, and excellent vision, they are well adapted for hunting.

When threatened they perform a convincing aggressive display. The neck frill is rapidly flared out while the lizard hisses and lunges with mouth agape. If this does not convince the predator to leave the Dragon alone, it will turn tail and flee on two legs.

Anyone considering keeping Frilled Dragons should be aware of the legal issues surrounding this lizard. As was stated previously, Australia does not export its fauna. That means that all specimens in the hobby should have come from New Guinea stock. This is a sticky issue. Unscrupulous or unknowing dealers can say that their Frilleds came "from Germany," but that often means they were smuggled from Australia and routed through Germany. Such lizards are illegal and can cause you a lot of trouble, particularly if you have any plans on producing and selling young. The young of illegally-smuggled animals are also illegal. They can be seized, you can be fined, you can be sent to jail. If you are planning on

Baby Frilleds are becoming more commonly available at reptile shows. Set up the terrarium before you purchase the lizard to help ease the transition.

purchasing a Frilled Dragon, you must make every effort to obtain animals who originated in New Guinea. Irian Jaya (an Indonesian territory occupying half of New Guinea) currently farm-raises Frilled Dragons for export. These animals and their offspring are the only legal Frilleds in the pet trade.

HOUSING

The housing of Frilled Lizards presents something of a challenge. Like the Bearded Dragons, Frilled Dragons are big and have a high activity level. A fairly tall cage is recommended, as these lizards enjoy climbing and seem to feel more secure when elevated. The minimum cage size would be about 55 gallons; a larger cage is strongly recommended. If you plan on housing a pair, you will need a cage at least the equivalent of a 100-gallon tank.

CAGE FURNISHINGS

With the Frilled Dragon, the substrate you use for the enclosure is not critical. Newspaper works well, as will any of the packaged reptile barks. Playground sand and cactus soil are fine and lend a natural look to the

This Frilled Dragon has a damaged snout, possibly from being kept in too small a cage.

terrarium. However, the lizard's constant racing about may kick up a lot of dust. Frilleds usually do not burrow, so the depth of the substrate need only be a couple of inches.

Climbing branches are a necessity. Frilleds really enjoy elevated perches. Provide a sturdy perch for each lizard. The branches should be at least the same thickness as the lizard. One or more perches should be placed beneath the basking light to allow natural basking behaviors. Rocks are not necessary, but certainly no harm will be done by including a few. Besides, they are attractive and can be used to help anchor the branches.

To prevent accidents involving falling branches, it is probably best to fasten the branches in place. If using a wire cage of some sort, simply tying the branches to the sides with wire will work. With a plastic or glass cage, you should probably use aquarium-safe silicone sealant. When using this product, work in a well-ventilated area and don't put the lizards in the enclosure until the fumes have completely dissipated, usually at least 24 hours. Read the package instructions carefully.

Many Frilled Dragons will not use a hide box. Some keepers, therefore, would say one is not needed. We feel that no harm is done by including one, especially when your Dragons first arrive. It will give them a secure refuge in the early stressful days. If they don't use it, you can remove it. You may want to try using an elevated hidebox. A large bird nesting box would be easy to attach to a branch or the side of the cage. These boxes are available at many pet stores.

More so than Bearded Dragons, Frilleds like water. A large bowl must be provided. Make sure it is heavy enough to resist efforts to spill it. A cat litter pan with a couple of heavy rocks in it for stability may be the way to go. Be prepared to clean the bowl thoroughly at least once a day; Frilleds are very fond of defecating in their water.

Hygiene must be strictly observed. Remove fecal matter every day. The substrate will probably need replacing every other month, depending on what substrate you use and how many Frilleds occupy the cage. This is a good time to strip the cage and disinfect the furnishings. Soak branches, rocks, shelters, and bowls in a bleach solution for at least half an hour. Scub off any fecal matter that happens to be present (for obvious reasons, keep sponges, rags, and towels used to clean reptiles separate from those used to clean humans). Wipe the interior of the cage with the bleach solution. Rinse the cage and all furnishings well. Dry everything off and replace the Dragons.

HEATING AND LIGHTING

Frilled Dragons require similar heating and lighting as Bearded Dragons, because, like the Beardeds, Frilleds in the wild spend a great amount of time soaking up the sunlight. Full-spectrum fluorescent lighting is a must. Frilleds must have access to UV light for several hours each day. This will help prevent metabolic bone disease and allow the lizards to look their best. Plant bulbs do not provide the correct wavelengths of light; use a bulb designed specifically for reptiles.

Frilled Dragons prefer the air temperature to be around 85°F; the basking site should reach a temperature of about 90-95°F. Night-time temperatures can be in the mid to upper 70's. A timer would be a wise investment. Since these lizards spend much of their time up in the branches, heat pads and hot rocks will be wastes of money.

Feeding the Frilled Dragon

Generally speaking, Frilled Dragons are aggressive eaters. They regard any small moving object as potential food. Because of this, the keeper must provide them with a variety of nutritious prey. In the wild, Frilled Dragons mainly eat insects and other arthropods, but they will eat lizards, snakes, eggs, birds, and small mammals if given the opportunity.

WHAT AND HOW MUCH

In captivity, some attempt must be made to give Frilled Dragons the variety they crave. Crickets, mealworms, waxworms, and mice are available at many pet stores. Some also carry earthworms that can be added to the diet occasionally. If available, grasshoppers and cockroaches are good food suitably sized for adult Frilleds. Always make sure that the prey offered is smaller than the lizard's head. Collecting insects from pesticide-free areas will provide some additional variety to the diet.

Remember that these lizards are very active and require a nutrient-rich diet. Crickets and mealworms should be gut-loaded before feeding them to the lizards. This is the only way to be sure that your Dragon's prey provides a balance of nutrients.

Frilled Dragons benefit from vitamin and mineral supplementation. Give hatchlings and juveniles up to six months old supplements every other feeding. Juveniles up to two years old can have supplements two or three times a week. When your Frilled is two years old and older, give it supplements twice a week.

Frilled Dragons eat a lot. You can expect an adult to consume a dozen crickets a day or a like amount of other prey. Young Frilleds will consume a proportionately larger amount of smaller prey. Obesity is not common in Frilleds because of the high levels of activity these lizards maintain. However, mice, especially pinkies and fuzzies, are high in fat and should only be fed to Frilleds occasionally.

RAISING INSECTS

Given that Frilled Dragons consume so much food, you may want to propagate some insects on your own. This will save you some money, so if you have the space and the time, it is probably a good idea. Crickets and mealworms are probably the easiest insects to raise.

Mealworms require very little space to raise. You will need a shallow container (a lid is not necessary except for your peace of mind), a few small pieces of burlap or other cloth, food (wheat bran, oat meal, alfalfa pellets, and/or flake fish food, along with some bits of fruits and vegetables for moisture and vitamins), and mealworms. Place the food in the container to a depth of 2-3 inches. Put some bits of fruit or vegetables on top (apples, potatoes, carrots, and yams are good); these will need to be changed about every other day. Lay the burlap on top of the fruit and *lightly* moisten. The mealworms can be dumped under the burlap.

If kept at room temperature, the mealworms will mature into beetles and breed. Watch closely for any signs of mold. If mold occurs, start a new colony with the mealworms and beetles from the old one. In any case, the colony will need to be cleaned out and restarted roughly every other month. King mealworms are a tropical species and are more difficult to raise.

Crickets are not quite as easy, but still simple enough. The major drawback is that they need to be heated. The use of a low-wattage incandescent light or small heat pad will be adequate. Fish tanks make good cricket containers. A 10-gallon will be fine. Place 2-3" of potting soil on the bottom of the tank. This should be *barely* moist. High humidity will cause fungus, cricket-death, and unpleasant odor. Add some crumpled newspaper or egg-crates to provide the crickets with hiding surfaces.

Crickets eat almost anything. Wheat bran, oatmeal, crushed corn flakes, rodent chow, and rabbit pellets all make a good diet. Add some moist fruits and vegetables. These should be replaced daily. Food should be placed in a shallow dish; keep the fruit separate from the dry items. Now add the crickets and let them do their thing. You will probably need to replace the egg-crates occasionally and clean out the substrate every other month or so. Keep the crickets clean to avoid transferring pathogenic bacteria to your pets.

Index

Photo Credits

Marian Bacon – p. 36
R. D. Bartlett – p. 4, 10, 15, 17, 20, 27, 29, 59
Isabelle Francais – p. 5, 8, 9,12, 19, 21-26, 28, 30, 33-35, 38-42, 44-48, 50, 51, 54
U. E. Friese – p. 6
G. & C. Merker – p. 1, 14, 37, 39, 49
G. & W. Merker – p. 3
J. Merli – p. 43
Robert G. Sprackland – p. 7, 32
Karl H. Switak – p. 18, 57
Z. Takacs – p. 13
John C. Tyson – p. 18, 31
D. Zoffer – p. 60